Making The House Fall Down

Beatrice Hawley

CONTENTS

I

The Rag-Picker   9
Psyche   10
The Painter   11
The Potter   12
The Travel Artist   13
Nightwalking   14
The Elect   15
The Cleaning Lady Thinks of Lizzie Borden   16
Rules for the Cleaning Lady   17
At the Clinic   18

II

Eclipse   21
Venice, 1949   22
Dream Poem   23
Moving   24
White Tents   26
The Ship   27
The Lovers   28
Evening   29
The Lemon-House   30
Small Stones   31
The First Mother   32
Eggs   33
Hiding   34
Nocturne   35
Spy   36
Stolen Poem   37
Mountains   38
Snapshot   39
The Visit   40

Gifts   41
The Mother's Poem   42
The Wife's Poem   43
Elizabeth Disguised as a Dancer   44
Blue Walls   45

III

The Picnic   49
Spring Poem   50
In the World   51
The Marsh   52
Nauset Beach   53
Swimming at Night   54
A Distance from Drowning   55
Summerhouse   56
Hibernation   57
Mount Auburn Cemetery   59
Stones   60
Jamaica Plain Poem   62
Love   63

I

THE RAG-PICKER

The woman who walks along the streets
is the woman collecting rags.
They fly to her from windows:
flags, silks, bridal sheets.

She is taller than the gates,
tucks her elbows in to shout.
She bundles everything and takes
it all home to her hills.

At night she comes back wearing her cloak,
the magic rings tight against her cheeks
make her mouth bloody as she leans
over the beds of children asleep.

THE POTTER

You get clay
red clay, from the potter
who hunches down
at the river's edge
near a large city.

He makes each pot perfect
he rolls them out to dry
under the sun. They bake.

After the river dries
the city moves to another delta.

The clay becomes motes of dust
dancing in your room
when you are a little girl
waking up from your nap.

You figure this out,
grown woman with clay
dusting your hair red.

THE TRAVEL ARTIST

Your thinning hair
wreathed in flowers, you
want a white house
near blue water.

Your family, a collection
of rich people, wave you
over oceans to settle
you down to earth.

You write letters to them:
"fire, fire, fire, fire,
my mail is censored the chief
of police is looking this way."

At night you shudder in your
new bed, you spill wine over
the sheets, you pull them
up to your chin.

NIGHTWALKING

You wear your skirt
like a flag you are
using to keep the lions back.

Little traps of thread
form like birds behind you.

You walk as if
you could dance on water.

Your angel shrugs down feathers
to cover the stars in your hair.

All over town mothers of men
are crying when you go by.

THE ELECT

His hand can shatter
as much as a cow
standing in green crystal.

His voice can speak
and teapots pour out
alone to fill a ravine.

His hair is flutes,
the better mayor.
His following tuck
chickens under their arms.

THE CLEANING LADY THINKS
OF LIZZIE BORDEN

In summer it gets hot.
The cleaning lady thinks of Lizzie Borden.
She carries clothes to hang on the line;
she knows air and sun will dry them better.

The house behind her has many rooms.
She has cleaned them each in turn.
There is a barn here too, and a pear tree;
but there is no axe and the pears rot.

She hangs the boy's jeans.
She hangs the father's shirt.
She hangs the mother's nightgown.
Her arms ache.

The people who live in this house are not her parents.
The boy makes lemonade for her,
at the end of the day she gets money;
no one here wills her the slightest harm.

The cleaning lady has heard
that Lizzie, awaiting trial, day after day
would squeeze an egg—which would not break:
the matron told the story to the court.

In the hot kitchen the glass of lemonade
waits on the clean table. The cleaning lady
touches the cold beads to her cheek,
she knows if she tried to squeeze an egg, it would break.

RULES FOR THE CLEANING LADY

Brush the twigs out of your hair if you live in a cave.
Enter quietly.
Love the animals in the house.
Don't feed the fish.
Never drink anything but one can of Diet Cola.
Eat one tuna salad sandwich on bread, not toast.
Ask for more vacuum cleaner bags.
If you bring a book hide it under a towel in the bathroom.
Read nowhere else.
Sit nowhere else.
Leave quietly.

You will be rewarded in heaven
where angels are even now weaving tapestries
to line the walls of your cave.

AT THE CLINIC

We are still.
We look very much the same
as we did a week ago.
The weight in our bodies
is only the weight of a small stone.
Today we will hold
our hands together;
our eyes will hook
into each other:
we will rub each other's backs
and draw our knees up
under our chins.

On the way home on the same bus
our eyes will unlock.
These days teach us
how to be fierce, how to hold
on to ourselves.

II

ECLIPSE

A boy limping across a field,
to a barn of darkening cracks;
flowers closed at noon.

Under the house
animals are hidden:
clustered, organized, terrible.

VENICE, 1949

The houses are sinking
no faster than before.
Beautiful women are still
buying gold, wearing it
on their arms.
She sells her rings, like the others.
Her daughters are in the country,
they are in the laps of nuns,
they are eating white grapes, they are dying.

But she is better off
than the Princess of Estonia,
who sleeps next door
in her shiny black dress,
all the emeralds gone.
She has a passport, she can travel,
she can buy medicine,
she can go to Philadelphia.
Her daughters will be cured,
she will buy them snowsuits.

DREAM POEM

KATE dreams a fish,
its tail wound down her back;
the shawl her mother made
over and over one whole summer.

JOHN dreams a hole:
water, well, mirror,
his white hand reaches his white hand—
O! He is a boy. His father is laughing.

BEATRICE dreams a little boat,
the little boat of children who drown
one after another, she can see
the stars in their hair.

These dreamers row
into the dreams they sleep
in the same house,
they will be tied past morning.

MOVING

We are getting ready to move
to a place near water:
small boats with lanterns,
prows up-turned, spearfishing.
The moon is continuous here,
houses made of lava,
fish drying in moonlight:
silver flakes on the path.

Beyond the antipodes
where light bends
and you can see it
my room has walls of blue chalk,
my floor is brown paper.
People lie on the paper
making outlines of angels:
each person makes a different angel
each angel covers a different person
even small children
are angel-covered.

There are peaches here,
there is jam to eat in winter
with tinned milk when it rains.
It is not far:
grandmothers may come and visit,
cousins can find work,
children learn the language quickly.
We are all going soon,
we will arrive early;
it will be morning
we will rub our eyes
we will see, see the land rise.

WHITE TENTS

Children in foreign countries
sleep under white tents
in summer.

Windows are left open,
voices come from the garden,
the voices of ghosts
who speak another language.

By day, during naps,
the country beyond the bed
is golden and the voices
more quiet than at night.

The mothers and fathers
do not know as they pull
the netting shut that the children,
safe from malaria,
are haunted.
They tell the children a story
of how the pots and pans in the kitchen
have dances at midnight.
When they leave the room
the children wait quietly
under the tents of mist
for the flowers and trees in the garden,
so much more alive,
to finally steal them.

THE SHIP

They are too high to see their eyes in the water.
The deck is a plain, and in the inner dining hall
the children are at table to eat more cake
            than they have seen.

The sea is darker than the ship above it.
The children's parents are walking about,
arms around each other like the old days
            before the journey.

This is the ship that takes the family home,
rocking them in her great belly .as she moves
so surely to the other side of the water
            where they will land.

THE LOVERS

Be patient. They were young together:
she with her lawn-party hat,
he with his tennis-playing sweater.

They've been together for years.
It would take too long
to tear up the bedspread she made
loving every stitch of the way.

If there is a stain on it now,
he's been blind to it for centuries.
In the morning they find
each other under it,
their bones tangled together.

EVENING

The inside of the shell
is our mother's room.
Into this room
our father comes at night
taking the coins
out of his pocket.

In the next room
my sisters and I are sleeping.
We take turns
waking in very dark
to hear the steady breathing;
without us it would stop.

Around the house
the moon pulls up the
seeds our mother planted.
All day my sisters and I
will weed her garden.
When our father comes home
the day will be over again.

THE LEMON-HOUSE

In a garden full of ghosts
threads hang from the almond tree.
You are a child here
with a new place to hide every day.

The pots which hold the lemon trees
are bigger than you.
In winter they are wheeled into the lemon-house
where dry leaves pile
under the chimney.

You hide there one night:
the grown-ups are having a party.
In the morning your father finds you
and without speaking cradles you
and takes the twigs out of your hair
one by one .

SMALL STONES

Our mother lies on her throne of cushions,
we climb up to her room
on a dangerous ledge.
We carry them in our mouths,
keeping the balance;
our hands make marks on the sill.
We take turns bringing
small stones for her eyes.

THE FIRST MOTHER

Your arms pulled down the sky.
I was just
a high-strung child to mind:
a fingernail, a pale moon,
a white shell,
my thin skin
stretched tight over the pulse.

You set me down near stones and water,
taught the crayfish how to move
and me how to hold still.

You were a mountain,
picking me up with one arm.
All the way home
I could feel your secrets
rolling against my knees.

EGGS

My mother
puts many eggs in her food
eggs are gold and silver to her,
they are treasures, they make
people see in the dark,
they make you smart in school.

I learn to swallow the yolk,
whole, to hold my breath,
to slide it down my throat.
All day I feel the knot
in my chest. I am not smart
in school. At night I am blind.

HIDING

I hide in the almond tree.
I am watching my mother
moving around the garden
with her silver scissors,
cutting flowers. She does
not see me. I see the glint
from the blades even when
my eyes are closed.

NOCTURNE

My sisters are writing at the kitchen table.
My father is washing my mother's hair.
I am upstairs looking out the window.
The salt marsh darkens.
I fill my bed with animals.

SPY

I am early.
No one is home.
When I am alone in the house
I do not know who I am.

I go upstairs.
I look in my mother's top drawer:
the nylon stockings are rolled up.
The scarves are folded.
Under the paper that lines the drawer
there is only wood.

STOLEN POEM

I used to climb out of the back window,
I used to walk towards the marsh out back;
I used to walk towards the salt smell.
My shoes used to fill with water.
I used to get cold.

I used to do this at night,
I used to bless the sleeping house
in summer more than winter. I used to
fill my mouth with pennies;
I used to do this quietly.

I used to come back cold and smelly.
I used to steal back into the house.
The animals used to stay asleep,
The sleepers would not turn in their beds.

MOUNTAINS

Though I stand on mountains
I cannot find my body.
She is washed down by water,
she is missing.
From a long way up
there is no sign,
no red jacket,
no hair making its own rivers.

I have been looking for weeks in these hills.
No one has seen a sign of her.
Not for years on years.
Without my body
I am only light
breaking nothing.

SNAPSHOT

My young mother stands
at the top of the stairs.
This is before I am born.
She will run into the arms
of my father who is not in this picture.

Her crocheted cap
fell into my hands.
She counted on each loop
of tiny beads. She wore it
to greet my father, it kept
her hair down tight.

THE VISIT

You come in.
You take the combs out of your hair.
You take off your red beads.
Your skirt is a tent.
Your blouse is a kite.

The children hide in the tent.
You and I run with the kite
we lose it in the high branches.
Be careful.
I am planning to steal your beads.

GIFTS

Everything is a gesture
towards your faces,
those great masks with eyes
that burn the heart.
We spend our lives
making you smile:
we do it to make you happy.

We wave colors to make you glad.
Our whole lives we bring nothing
but every scrap
of treasure we can find.

We bring water:
you love the sea.
We bring branches:
you love houses.
We bring rags:
you love costumes.

All over the world
we are planning bank robberies
and christenings
for just one smile.

It's nothing
we do it to make you happy
our whole lives.

THE MOTHER'S POEM

One by one the lights go out.
You want to join them,
tuck your head under and sleep.
Already the dreamers
are joining each other in fields,
already they call you,
urging you under their blankets.

You are still awake.
You see your white gown,
a flag in the window.
The dreamers under their trees
eating their night picnics
never pull you in.

THE WIFE'S POEM

The animals are asleep,
the children are covered,
the mother is standing in the hall
leaning her arms into the sky.
She can't sleep. She watches
the dark spaces crack with light.

The husband is moaning.
He is having a nightmare about lions.
Her hand is there, soothing
him over to a dream of water.
She knows this will not last:
she will break or learn to sleep.

Her hand in the future will be settling
small things down in their corners,
folding a narrow blanket,
hemming thin curtains
for the room with one window only
she will live in alone.

ELIZABETH DISGUISED AS A DANCER

I see your embroidered legs,
I see the dance you imagined,
I see the sparks on your toes.
You are moving faster than I can
see. I touch the scrap of cloth
you left in my drawer.
I see it crumble: you are
faster away than what you left here.
I see the threads form themselves,
I see them into your cloak,
your disguise on my table.
I see the invisible motion,
I see your dust turn to silk,
fluttering in the cracks of my floor.
I see you scattered in my pockets,
I see you moving again.

BLUE WALLS

Now you are free to wander in the night
through every corner of the house;
your fingers remember every dark shape.
You lie in your mother's bed and
learn that blue, after all, is only a color,
easy to match, a soothing backdrop
to her insomnia, to her migraine.

Mother was not well. She was in bed.
The blue blanket was folded at her feet.
You had to be very quiet in those times,
you took your shoes off at her door. You played
all by yourself for hours in the linen closet
near the smooth pile of blue towels,
you played being dead covered with talcum powder.

You have grown. It is true you have learned
we live in a human world together;
we have all been lost in our mother's houses
we have all crept down in the night
to put something sweet in our mouths.
You look out from the high windows, now,
and can see other houses, other lights gleaming.

III

THE PICNIC

We are reaching the landing
where we see spread
the wine and chicken:
this is the French
picnic where you imagined
a boy standing to count stars
he fixed near water.

Behind the scene is another.
Someone is singing
the boy to sleep.
She is his mother.
His head is on her lap,
the cave of his dreams.
Her dress spreads
a cloud on the lawn.

We move back
and see the ring of trees
which keeps the wolves away.

SPRING POEM

for John

The city is behind us.
The river is before us.
We walk over the bridge.
Now the edge of the river looks
like the edge of the river at Agincourt:
I tell you the English are winning.

You say these are cliffs.
You are a giant stepping over
chasms, seeking the monster
who sleeps underneath.

This year your first stone
skips five times.
Last year's last stone
skipped twice.

The next bridge takes us back.
The side we cross to now is edged
by yellow stones, stones glowing
with minerals, chemicals, some kind of poison.
We are used to this crossing:
halfway we always stop to count the boats.

Again this year you cry
when we get to the street.
You say you are crying because
a paper cup in the gutter is alone.

IN THE WORLD

I sit on the floor
near the cage
where a naked woman is keening.
The woman has killed
a little boy.
"He wouldn't stop crying
and I pushed the pillow
on his face to hush him. Now
they say he died
on the way to the hospital.
My boy Chris had to call
the police."

I have nothing to give
but my hand through the bars
which she grips
black-and-blue.

Later, in my own room
at the top of my house
I will sit alone
and very still.

THE MARSH

You make yourself new again.
Along your side,
only a thin line marks the scar
where you lay open one whole summer.

Steam rises from your body
in this heat.
You move slowly
you sit up to your chin in yourself.

One morning you are a blue floor.
You are rising, you are learning
to walk again, your feet do not stumble
over the wide roots.

The birds come back,
they tear at you, opening their beaks
in hunger, you feed them.
They will stay.

Again the salt burns in your blood,
but your mud is soft
and you are walking towards the sea.

NAUSET BEACH

From this nest of sand
she could watch clouds all day.
Or, looking straight,
past the ocean, find land
where salt fields wait
for the women to arrive.

Bending to gather the salt,
the women talk,
their cheeks gleam like diamonds;
making hard light skim over the water
but she cannot hear them.

Tonight she will put back
the salt from her hair,
the sea may carry it there,
all the way over:
the women are always waiting
for every grain to rest.

SWIMMING AT NIGHT

The water carries the body
as it carries other simple beasts:
otter, bear, salmon.

The eyes see only the rainbows
lights from the porches make
on the dark water.

The porches are human—
voices carry over the water,
they are planning to pick berries.

The body in the water smiles as it
turns itself over to float
before it turns to go home.

A DISTANCE FROM DROWNING

A hand can remember
how it feels to be lost
in folds of sand, in the
way water beats
over and over
to your drowning scene.

When dragged under, kick.
Pull up sharp to where the gold
brings ladders to the cave of water;
follow the spear of light.

When you save yourself
they let you tell stories
up and down the beach
all night on the porches
of the fish restaurants.

SUMMERHOUSE

This is the outcome of looking
down the dark lawn
towards the black water.
The trees lean, a slow
shadow adrift on the lake
moves with a light of its own.
I am holding the railing
and the touch of dreams
crouches in my fingers:
this is night blindness.

Summer nights I am always alone.
The rising dusk is over.
It is dark now.
I move towards the water
and my walking is slow.

The water is eating the rocks.
No one is here.
If I live through this
I will live forever.

HIBERNATION

like a secret which spins on alone
lying under oceans of snow
your fingers are weaving lace
your eyes are closed by dreams
you think everything you imagine
will occur in pairs

all around you pairs
of shadows which you alone
are observing I can't imagine
so much solace in dreams
like a cloud of lace
the intricate patterns of snow

moving as still as snow
an old woman wears lace
watching geese fly in pairs
you are charmed by her dreams
and cannot leave her alone
she is replacing all you imagine

later I try and imagine
how it would be if the lace
which covers you was actually snow
which gives nothing in pairs
each flake always alone
fastening you like a hook to dreams

then all your dreams
would be easier to imagine
you would not be alone
every thought would change the lace
every change would break the pairs
and over everything would ride the snow

after all the snow
insinuates into dreams
the irrelevance of pairs
would change everything you could imagine
and the cloak of intricate lace
would remind you of being alone

there are pairs you cannot imagine
even as snow begins to lace
up the dreams which made you alone

MOUNT AUBURN CEMETERY

We are in the trees around you.
(This narrow path, the trees close,)
You could touch us, now.
You are in Mount Auburn Cemetery.
The city below is in the cup of a spoon
and the trees are huge. They stand in your path.
Auburn is the color of hair you cannot buy.
Henna-rinse is an enamel basin. Hair grows
after you are dead. The scalp burns.
(moss growing on stones as though
   arranged for a creche in Italy.)
Those who believed, saw us.
Your day will be in the country
pricked by the cold trees;
it will remind you that you must suffer
to be beautiful.
(The cemetery is like a park,
   a wide green space at the edge
   of a city. A place where frogs sleep.)
These foolish animals lie down
only to feed us.

STONES

These stones have not been arranged.
In the country of monuments along every path,
this is the border along the coast,
these are the leavings from the mountain of angels.
The dolphins who copy the angels are sleeping
they do not see me bruise my feet.

When I come here there is no moon.
The stones must be ordered by remembering
light cast by dancers. I cannot find the stone
with only the memory of a streetlamp miles away.
I use my hands to test the weight of each,
I move down closer. I touch them with my tongue.

They taste salt. I believe in mineral properties.
When I find the right monument I will taste it.
I will swallow it, I will carry it in my belly.
I will never drown. The marble will not sink.
I will be buried near water. My hair will grow
when I die, a tree will bloom from my eyes.

The one will be right that holds the light
from the body of a young swimmer who drowned.
The stone will seem at home among the others,
these others that pretend to be children
playing at the water's edge. They are liars.
They are old men who fell out of little boats.

They are old fishermen who never swam:
they hate the sea. The sea is a machine
with long chains to pull them in.
The sea is a machine which rubs them together;
they are polished, gleaming, they are like babies—
if I could see, they would trick me.

Every night I come here and put new stones in my mouth.
Every night the new stones fail me.
In the morning I am never invisible.
I always have to go back along the road,
the fishermen greet me on their way
to the small boats, their eyes are full of light.

JAMAICA PLAIN POEM

We are not dancing
in Leopoldville, on the veranda.
If anything, even there, we would
have had our noses pressed to the windows
looking at the dance floor littered
with broken flowers:
bougainvillea, orchid, gardenia.

Or, leaving the picture palace
we would have walked down the hill
past the Parker House Hotel
where there are no windows,
only a whiff of rolls people eat every day,
not just on Thanksgiving.

We would have gone home on the trolley
to your house in Jamaica Plain,
the house set in, apart from the others,
small and with a real yard.
Your mother and father on the porch
would have greeted us smiling.

Today we break the bread between us.
You tell me stories about Jamaica Plain,
about calling your porch a veranda.
I take the stories into my life.

LOVE

like wisteria
choking the house, pulling
the porch off,
making the foundation crazy

grey in the off season
letting you think the birch trees
will make shelter

but the root will not burn out,
the vine comes back
making the house fall down
under the sweetest flower